MICRO
CHAPBOOK
SCI-FI RPG

DELUXE CORE RULEBOOK

D0764677

Ultra Simple Rules for Solo
Roleplaying in a Grim Sci-Fi World
Designed by Noah Patterson

Find us on DriveThru RPG!

Image Citations

Cover Art: © Dean Spencer Art used with permission
Section 6.0 Art: © Maciej Zagorski used with permission
Section 6.1 Art: © Maciej Zagorski used with permission
Section 14.0 Art: © Peter Saga used with permission
Section 21.0 Art: © Jack Badashski, 2016 used with permission
Section 22.0 Art: © Jack Badashski, 2016 used with permission

All other art was taken from the public domain.

STOP!

DON'T BUY THIS BOOK!
At least, not yet.

The basic rules for the Micro Chapbook Sci-Fi RPG system can be downloaded for FREE in any Micro Chapbook through DriveThruRPG.com. Each stand alone Chapbook includes the complete rules for you to play the game.

With that in mind, this Deluxe Edition Core Rulebook also contains all the rules you need to play the game plus a few additions. You'll notice subtle differences here and there-- but overall the game is the same one you've come to know and differences are noted in **BOLD** or with a **Gameplay Note.**

Even with the subtle differences, this book is completely compatible with ANY and ALL Chapbook Scenarios. In fact, this book includes a "Mission Generator" for various types of scenarios. After that you can download any number of the free products in the Micro Chapbook line for further scenarios and adventures.

Contents

1.0: What is Micro Chapbook Sci-Fi RPG?
2.0: What Do I Need To Play?
3.0: Gameplay Basics
4.0: Character Creation
5.0: Character Stats
6.0: Character Classes
7.0: Character Ranks
8.0: Health and Willpower
9.0: Weapons
10.0: Armor and Items
11.0: Generating Rooms
12.0: Doorways
13.0: Room Types
14.0: Aliens
15.0: Combat Procedure
16.0: Bravery
17.0: Ranged Combat
18.0: Melee Combat
19.0: Running Away
20.0: Search Rolls
21.0: The Boss Alien
22.0: Backtracking
23.0: Leveling Up
24.0: Away Missions
25.0: Playing with a Game Master

Section 1.0

What is a Micro Chapbook Sci-Fi RPG?

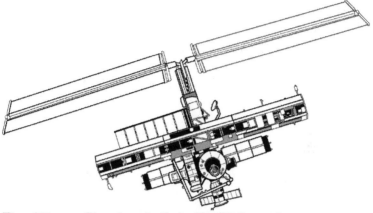

The Micro Chapbook Sci-Fi RPG system is an ultra simple roleplaying game that can be played solo or with a traditional GM if you so wish.

The main game focuses on solitaire gameplay, starring a single interplanetary explorer on missions for the Galactic Space Force. It uses randomly generated scenarios to make each game session a little different. This book also includes a random mission generator.

The universe for this game is brutal, unforgiving, and dark. Expect to die and die often.

Section 2.0

What Do I Need to Play?

In order to play Micro Chapbook Sci-Fi RPG you will need to gather the following easy-to-find items:

2 six-sided dice
A sheet or notepad of graph paper (or a game mat with a grid)
A Character Sheet (or note paper)
A pencil with a good eraser
These rules or any stand alone chapbook scenario.
Extra scenarios and modules (optional).
Micro Chapbook RPG game supplements (optional).

Section 3.0

Gameplay Basics

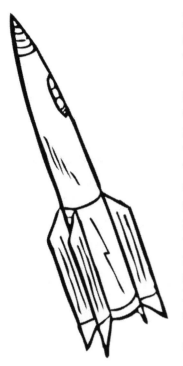

During gameplay, you almost always roll 1D6, trying to score equal to or LOWER than your stat score. If your character is proficient in the stat being tested, roll 2 dice and take the better result of the 2. 1 always succeeds. 6 always fails. This mechanic is used for all tasks including attacking, avoiding obstacles, hacking doors, and most everything else.

The only time this is different is when you roll for damage (either when dealing weapon damage or taking damage from an alien or obstacle). Some damage scores may ask you to roll 1D3. When you see 1D3 it means you roll a single D6 and half the result rounding up.

Section 4.0

Character Creation

Character creation is completed in 5 very simple steps:

1. Determine The 4 Stat Scores.
2. Choose a Character Class.
3. Choose a Character Rank.
4. Determine Your Starting Health and Willpower.
5. Roll for Credits and Purchase Items.

Each step is explained in further detail in the following sections.

Section 5.0

Character Stats

Your character has 4 main statistics:

Strength (ST): Used for melee attacks and breaking down doors.

Dexterity (DE): Used for ranged attacks and avoiding obstacles.

Wits (WI): Used for hacking doors and science related tasks.

Charisma (CH): Used for increasing your Willpower and showing your bravery.

During character creation you are granted 7 points to assign between the 4 stats as you see fit. No stat can have a score lower than 1 or higher than 4 during this step, but these may be altered later on.

Section 6.0

Character Classes

There are 4 Character Classes to Choose From. Each one will make you proficient in one stat.

SOLDIER:

Soldiers are adept at hand to hand combat and similar ST based tests.

Most starships are assigned either a single high ranking soldier to help consult and offer advice if a combat situation occurs, or a squad of soldiers to fight off aliens if the ship is boarded.

They are proficient in Strength.

RANGER:

Rangers are adept at long range combat and DE based tests.

Most starships have a ranger or squad of rangers to assist in space combat. They also are equipped to accompany away teams to any planet's surface to help guard and protect the scientists and technicians while their work is being done.

They are proficient in Dexterity.

TECH:

Techs are adept at solving puzzles, foreseeing traps and ambushes, hacking computers, and similar WI based tests.

Most starships have a lead technician who handles all the ship's computer inputs and outputs. They are also often scientists, in charge of biology and collecting alien plant and animal samples from different planets. They are interested in research over combat, but won't shirk away from killing an enemy.

They are proficient in Wits.

DIPLOMAT:

Diplomats are socially savvy space explorers and are adept at holding onto their Willpower and Bravery in difficult situations.

Every starship is assigned a diplomat, someone specializing in languages and interacting with alien races.

They are proficient in Charisma.

Section 6.7

Crafting Your Own Class

If none of the given classes appeal to you, feel free to craft one of your own!

To do this is simple.

Think of any class you'd want to play as. What is their background, history, and skills? What proficiency would they have? Write in the class name and the Stat Proficiency on your sheet.

Section 7.0

Character Ranks

There are 4 Character Ranks to Choose From. Each one will grant you a +1 bonus in one stat.

SECURITY:
The Security Rank is all about safety and protection of the starship crew and humanity as a whole. They receive +1 in Strength.

ENGINEERING:
The Engineer Rank is all about nimble fingers able to fix any part of a starship at a moment's notice if it should break. They receive +1 in Dexterity.

SCIENCE:

The Science Rank is all about research, digging, and finding new and exciting things. They receive +1 in Wits.

COMMAND:

The Command Rank is about organization, order, and leadership. They are often in charge of away teams or even whole starships. They receive +1 in Charisma.

Section 7.1

Crafting Your Own Ranks

If none of the given ranks appeal to you, feel free to craft one of your own! To do this is simple. Think of any rank you'd want to play as. What is their background, history, and skills? What stat bonus would they have? Write in the rank name and the Stat bonus on your sheet.

Section 8.0

Health and Willpower

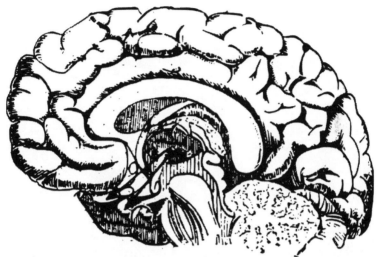

Your Health and Willpower are determined by your current stats.

Health: Your health is the total sum of your Strength + Dexterity + 20 (+10 for a challenge).

Willpower: Your will is the total sum of your Wits + Charisma + 20 (+10 for a challenge).

Section 9.0

Weapons

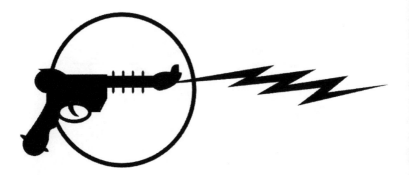

You're now getting close to finishing your character. All that is left is to roll up your starting Credits and purchase weapons, armor, and other items. Credits replace gold in this version of the system. If combining games, the currencies are interchangeable.

Roll 2D6 to determine your starting credits. Weapons are listed on the next page. Each has a damage rating and a cost (in credits). Some damages are listed as 1D2. This means rolls a D6. Odds = 1 and Evens = 2.

Melee Weapons			Ranged Weapons		
Name	Dmg	C	Name	Dmg	C
Dagger	1	1	Throwing Star	1	2
Rapier	1D2	2	Tranquilizer	1D2	3
Short Sword	1D3	3	Stun Gun	1D3	4
Long Sword	1D3+1	4	Stun Rifle	1D3+1	5
Great Sword*	1D3+2	5	Stun Cannon*	1D3+2	6
Hand Axe	1D3+1	4	Phaser MK 1	1D3+1	5
Great Axe*	1D3+2	5	Phaser MK 2	1D3+2	6
Vibro Dagger	2	2	Mini Lazer	2	3
Vibro Sword*	1D6	6	Blaster	1D6	7
Vibro Axe*	1D6+1	7	Phaser Rifle	1D6+1	8
Electric Mace	1D2	2	Electro Bolter	1D2	3
Electric Pole	1D3	3	Plasma Dart	1D3	4
Plasma Dagger*	1D6	6	Plasma Gun*	1D6	7
Plasma Sword*	2D6	12	Plasma Rifle*	2D6	13
Plasma Axe*	2D6+1	13	Plasma Cannon*	2D6+1	14

Weapons with the asterisk have the "Blow Through" ability and can deal damage to multiple enemies.

Section 10.0

Armor and Items

Armor grants the wearer a boost to their health, will, or both. Other items such and food and potions can be used to restore lost health and will. All items are consumable. They can be used at any point in the game, even during battle.

Each piece of armor and each item notes the bonus and the cost. The number in parentheses

to the left of each item name is used for
Search Rolls.

Armor			Items		
Name	Bonus	C	[*]Name	Bonus	C
Triton Fabric Uniform	+3H	1c	(2) K-Rations	1D3 H	1c
Comm Badge	+3W	1c	(3) Deblorian Ale	1D3 W	1c
Flux Shield	+6H	2c	(4) Stim Kit	1D6 H	2c
Cybernetic Uplink	+6W	2c	(5) Tranquilizer	1D6 W	2c
Personal Force Field	+6HW	3c	(6) Emergency Med Kit	FULL HW	6c

Section 11.0

Generating Rooms

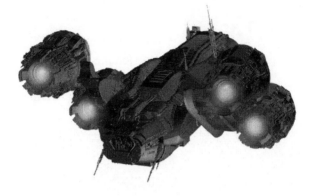

Begin the game by choosing a random square on the graph paper and generating the first room in the scenario (the **Entrance**).

To generate a room, roll 2D6. The number rolled in the number of squares in the room. These can be drawn in any way, shape, or form so long as they are orthogonally connected.

Next, roll 1D3 (1D6 divided by 2 rounded up). This is the number of new doors added in the room (in addition to any door you just used). Draw small rectangles to represent the doors along any single square's edge to designate an exit. Each time you move through a door you will generate a new room in this manner. The **Entrance** doesn't contain aliens.

In the following example, the player rolled 2 dice. One came up 6 and the other 4 for a total of 10. They then built a room of ten squares as so. Next, they rolled 1 die. The result was 6.

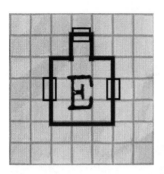 Divided in half that is 3. 3 doors. The player then drew in three smaller rectangles to designate where the doors in the room are located.

Finally, the player marks the first room with an E to show it is the Entrance/Exit of the scenario. A player may backtrack any time to the Entrance if the scenario gets too hard. However, they don't earn the extra credit bonus for killing the Boss!

GAMEPLAY NOTE: In the regular Micro Chapbooks, the rules instruct the player to only roll 1 die for room size. This book says to use 2. 2 dice simply offer more options, and it is up to you as the player to decide whether to roll 1 or 2 dice. I just suggest making it consistent throughout a single scenario.

Section 12.0

Doorways

When you leave the Entrance (or any room in the scenario once it has been cleared of aliens) you will choose 1 door in the room to move through. Before moving through, however, you will need to make a Door Roll. Roll 1D6 on the door chart provided in the scenario. Some scenarios will add new door results, but there are 4 absolute basic door options that could occur:

Unlocked: The door is unlocked and you may move through freely without stopping.

Stuck: The door appears to be stuck. Make a ST check to get through. If you fail you may lose 1 WILL to reroll and try again.

Locked: The door is locked. Make a WI check to pick the lock. If you fail you may lose 1 WILL to reroll and try again.

Malfunction: The electronic door has a malfunction. You must make a WI check to fix it and move through. If you fail, take 1D3 damage as the door blows up but still move through.

GAMEPLAY NOTE: Once a door has been moved through, shade the doorway in black to show that you no longer have to roll when using that door. (This just makes tracking easier)

If there are multiple doors in a room, you can choose to attempt one door. If you fail, you can choose a different one. Retrying any stuck or locked door always requires a Will loss. You MUST always make an attempt on a trapped door once you've rolled it up--as the trap catches you unawares as you are attempting to go through.

Section 13.0

Room Types

Each newly generated room you enter also has a Room Type that will make it slightly different from other rooms.

Upon entering a room, roll 1D6 on the scenario's Room Type chart. Each type will have a lettered code for you to write inside the room to remind you. Types include things like dirt or stone floors, water, or even crypts and tourture chambers.

Some rooms types only add flavor to the story, but most will either include a trap, an obstacle, or a die roll modifier (usually +1) for one stat that makes things harder for you.

Aliens

Every room has aliens (or enemies of some sort). After Entering any room and determining its type roll 1D6 on the scenario's alien chart to generate the aliens in the room.

Roll once to determine the alien type. Roll a second time to determine the number of that alien that appears in the room. Each alien has a Max number that can appear in a room. Even if you roll higher, only the Max number will appear and no more can appear than the number of squares in a room. Aliens also have a Health Damage (H-DMG), Willpower Damage (W-DMG), and Life Force (LF).

Section 15.0

Combat Procedure

The instant you run into any aliens, combat begins.

Combat in the Micro Chapbook RPG system is extremely simple and is completed in 3 easy steps.

1. **Bravery:** Check to see how brave you are.
2. **Ranged Combat:** If able, make a ranged attack against the aliens now.
3. **Melee Combat:** You MUST make a melee attack. Make a melee attack now.

Once all three steps are complete, start over from the top and repeat them all. Do this until all the aliens are defeated, you are killed, or you have elected to run away.

Section 16.0

Bravery

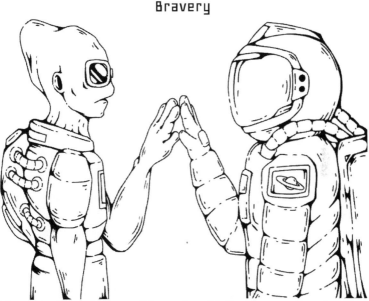

The sight of any alien, be it large or small, can invoke the deepest fear in even the bravest or explorers.

During the Bravery Step make a CH check. If you pass, gain 1 Willpower. If you fail, you lose Will according to the alien's W DMG (Usually you have to roll a die to see how much).

If your Will ever reaches 0, all rolls take a +1 modifier to the die result as your character is losing hope in their ability to succeed in their mission. (A natural roll of 1 STILL always succeeds despite this or any other modifier. Will mods stack with room mods). Even if you have 0 Will, always make the Bravery Check to see if you earn a Will back.

Section 17.0

Ranged Combat

IF (and only if) the current room is 4 squares or larger you may make a ranged attack. To make a ranged attack you must have a ranged weapon. Roll a DE stat check. If you succeed at the check, apply weapon damage to the alien's Life Force. (usually by rolling). Extra damage after an alien is defeated CAN'T roll over to other aliens in the room UNLESS the weapon has the "Blow Through" ability. You targeted a single alien with the attack.

Section 18.0

Melee Combat

During Melee Combat you MUST make a melee attack using a ST check. If you succeed, apply the weapon's damage to the alien's LF. (usually by rolling). Similarly, damage can't roll over to multiple enemies (unless you have the "Blow Through" ability). However, if you FAIL, one alien in the room deals damage to you. Roll the alien's H DMG and apply it to your health rating. If it reaches 0 you die.

Section 79.0

After ALL steps of combat you can elect to run away by making a CH check. If you fail, one alien in the room deals damage and another round of combat begins. If you pass choose any door in the room to escape through. If it is a door you haven't explored yet roll on the Doorway chart. If it is stuck or locked and you fail the roll, one alien in the room deals damage and combat resumes. If you escape, add a number to the room and record what aliens were left behind on a sheet of paper. They will be there if you return.

Section 20.0

Search Rolls

After you have cleared a room of all aliens roll 1D6. If you get a one through five you earn that many credits. Add it to your credit rating on the character sheet.

If you roll a six, roll on the Items chart in the section on armor and items. Each item is assigned a number. If you roll that number you find that item. If you roll a 1 on the items chart you find nothing.

Section 27.0

The Boss Aliens

Each scenario has its own boss (marked with a
* on the Alien Chart) The boss will not appear
until you've encountered all the other aliens
on the chart at least once. Additionally, the
boss will only appear in specific rooms, as

designated by the scenario. If you roll the boss when it can't appear, reroll. Once it is defeated, the game ends.

Section 22.0

Backtracking

At any point in the game you may work your way backwards and return to rooms you already visited. If you run away from a room, the aliens you left will still be there.

If you left the room empty, roll 1D6. On a roll of 6, new aliens appear. Roll for aliens as normal. Once you've defeated the aliens, make a Search Roll −2 to see if the aliens were carrying any. If the result is 0, you get no credits. You can't find items as the room has already been searched once.

Section 23.0

Leveling Up

After defeating a boss, count up the number of rooms you explored. **Earn 1 credit for each room. If you do not defeat the boss, you don't get the bonus.** In between games you may spend 100 credits to add +1 to one stat (50 credits for an easier game). No stat can be higher than 5. You may also buy new equipment. You may only have 1 melee and 1 ranged weapon at a time.

Section 24.0

Away Missions

The following section will give you all the tools you need to generate a random away mission scenario for the game. Creating a scenario is done in two steps:

1. **Determine Location:** Roll on the location chart to determine the location. Each location has its own Doorways table and Room Type table.
2. **Determine Hostiles:** Roll on the Hostiles chart. Each Hostile category has its own Alien Table.

For the purposes of this random mission generator, rooms where a boss can appear are marked with an asterisk.

Locations	
1	Hostage Ship (P 49)
2	Derelict Ship (P 50)
3	Oversized Asteroid (P 51)
4	Mining Rig (P 52)
5	Alien Ship (P 53)
6	Interdimensional Rift (P 54)

Hostiles	
1	Space Pirates (P 55)
2	Bugites (P 56)
3	Androids (P 57)
4	Martians (P 58)
5	Demonids (P 59)
6	Grenkins (P 60)

HOSTAGE SHIP

This ship has been taken hostage by an alien force.

Doorways		
5-6	Unlocked	Move through freely.
4	Stuck	ST Check
3	Locked	WI Check
1-2	Malfunction	WI Check or take 1D3 H-DMG

Room Types		
1	Corridor	C	An empty corridor. No Effect
2	Hull Breach	Br	This room has a hole in the hull. Make a DE check or take 1D3 damage.
3	Hostages	H	This room houses hostages. After clearing this room, you earn x2 credits
4	Med Bay	M	Make a WI check to gain 1D6 health.
5	Council Room*	Co	The MAX number of aliens is increased by 1.
6	Captain's Room*	Ca	This room has been taken over by the boss.

DERELICT SHIP

This ship has sat seemingly abandoned for years.

	Doorways	
5-6	Unlocked	Move through freely.
4	Stuck	ST Check
3	Locked	WI Check
1-2	Malfunction	WI Check or take 1D3 H-DMG

	Room Types		
1	Corridor	C	An empty corridor. No Effect
2	Darkness*	D	This room is dark. +1 on DE and ST rolls.
3	Chemical Leak*	Cl	Make a WI check or get stuck taking 1D3 damage.
4	Hull Breach	Br	This room has a hole in the hull. Make a DE check or take 1D3 damage.
5	No Gravity	G	This room has no gravity. +1 on DE rolls.
6	Crew*	Cr	Most of the original crew is in this room. They are all dead and rotting. +1 CH rolls.

OVERSIZED ASTEROID

This large asteroid houses a series of tunnels.

Doorways		
5-6	Open	Move through freely.
3-4	Blocked	ST Check
1-2	Cave In	WI Check or take 1D3 H-DMG

Room Types			
1	Passageway	P	An empty passage. No Effect
2	Darkness*	D	This room is dark. +1 on DE and ST rolls.
3	Icy	I	This room is covered in ice. +1 DE rolls.
4	Low Ceiling	Lc	This room has a low ceiling. +1 on ST rolls.
5	Hive*	H	This room has extra aliens in it. Add +1 to the # of aliens in here.
6	Wreckage*	Wr	The wreckage of a small ship is here. +1 to the Search Roll.

MINING RIG

This old planet mining rig has been out of operation for years.

Doorways		
5-6	Unlocked	Move through freely.
4	Stuck	ST Check
3	Locked	WI Check
1-2	Malfunction	WI Check or take 1D3 H-DMG

Room Types			
1	Corridor	C	An empty corridor. No Effect
2	Hull Breach	Br	This room has a hole in the hull. Make a DE check or take 1D3 damage.
3	Equipment Malfunction	E	The old mining equipment here is going haywire. Make a WI check to shut it down or take 1D3 damage.
4	Precious Metals*	P	This room houses mined metals. Any credits earned here are doubled.
5	No Gravity	G	This room has no gravity. +1 on DE rolls.
6	Smelter*	S	This room contains a metal smelter that still seems to be running. The heat is unbearable. Make a ST check or take 1D3 damage.

ALIEN SHIP

You've been ordered to board and infiltrate an alien ship.

Doorways		
5-6	Unlocked	Move through freely.
4	Stuck	ST Check
3	Locked	WI Check
1-2	Malfunction	WI Check or take 1D3 H-DMG

Room Types			
1	Corridor	C	An empty corridor. No Effect
2	Private Quarters*	P	+1 to Search Rolls.
3	Sick Bay	Sb	After clearing this room heal 1D3 health.
4	Engineering	E	The engines of the ship hum loudly. +1 WI and CH rolls.
5	Science Lab	Sl	Sick looking specimens float in cryo tanks. +1 CH rolls.
6	The Bridge*	B	The bridge computers have tons of strange alien symbols. +1 WI rolls.

INTERDIMENSIONAL RIFT

You've entered a strange labyrinth through a rift in space.

	Doorways	
5-6	Unlocked	Move through freely.
4	Stuck	ST Check
3	Locked	WI Check
2	Phase	The door phases in and out. Make a WI check or take 1D3 H-DMG.
1	Alive	The door is alive. ST Check or take 1D3 H-DMG

	Room Types		
1	Corridor	C	An empty corridor. No Effect
2	Spinning	S	This room seems to be spinning. +1 DE rolls.
3	UltaCrystal*	U	A strange crystal shows you your death. Make a WI check or take 1D6 W-DMG.
4	Flesh*	F	This room is made of pulsing flesh. Make a ST check or the walls begin to suck you in for 1D3 H-DMG.
5	Mirror	M	This room has mirrors that seem to see into infinity. Make a WI check or take 1D3 W-DMG.
6	Lair*	L	This strange room appears to be the lair of some alien. +1 CH rolls.

SPACE PIRATES

Space Pirates only care about one thing, killing to gain money.

#	Alien	Max	H-DMG	W-DMG	LF
1	Robotic Parrot	6	1	1	3
2	Cabin Boy	4	1D3	-	5
3	Pirate Gunner	3	1D3+1	1	7
4	Vibro Sword Swashbuckler	2	1D6	1D3	10
5	Second Mate	1	1D6	1D6	15
6	Pirate King*	1	1D6+1	1D6+1	25

BUGITES

A race of bug like aliens that lay eggs near humans as a food source

#	Alien	Max	H-DMG	W-DMG	LF
1	Exploding Eggs	6	1D6	0	1
2	Nat Swarm	6	1	1	1
3	Bug Hatchling	6	1D3	1D3	3
4	Bug Guard	4	1D3+1	1D3+1	5
5	Bug Warrior	3	1D3+2	1D3+2	7
6	Bug Queen*	1	1D6	1D6+1	25

ANDROIDS

Robots who once served man, but now have a will of their own.

#	Alien	Max	H-DMG	W-DMG	LF
1	Sentinel Bot	6	1	1	1
2	Turret Gun	6	1D6	1	1
3	Mechanic Android	6	1D3	1D3	3
4	Flamethrower Android	4	1D6	1D3+1	5
5	Assassin Android	3	1D6+1	1D3+2	7
6	Mother Brain*	1	1D3	2D6	15

MARTIANS

Aliens who lived beneath cloaked domes on mars for millennia

#	Alien	Max	H-DMG	W-DMG	LF
1	Martian Trainee	6	1	1	1
2	Martian Guard	5	1D2	1D2	5
3	Martian Gunner	4	1D3	1D3	7
4	Martian Rifleman	3	1D3+1	1D3+1	10
5	Martian Swordsmith	2	1D6	1D6	15
6	Martian Warlord*	1	1D6+1	1D6+1	20

DEMONIDS

Flesh eating aliens from the "Hell" dimension

#	Alien	Max	H-DMG	W-DMG	LF
1	Space Zombie	6	1	1	1
2	Fleshling	5	1	1D3	1
3	Fleshmonger	4	1D3	1D3+1	5
4	Hell Guard	3	1D6	1D6	10
5	Electric Horseman	2	1D6	1D6+1	15
6	Queen of the Hell Dimension*	1	1D6	2D6	30

GRENKINS

An all female race of green skinned beings.

#	Alien	Max	H-DMG	W-DMG	LF
1	Grenkin Squire	6	1D2	1D2	3
2	Grenkin Trainee	6	1D3	1D2	5
3	Grenkin Tactics Officer	5	1D3+1	1D2	7
4	Grenkin Security Officer	5	1D3+1	1D3	9
5	Grenkin Assassin	3	1D6	1D3	12
6	Grenkin Captain	1	1D6+1	1D6	25

Section 26.0

Playing With a Game Master

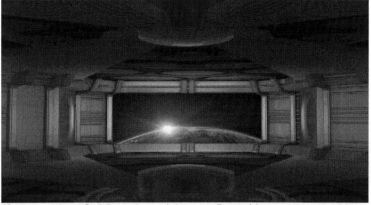

Using the following tips, play the game with a
traditional Game Master.

The GM can choose to pre build the
mission beforehand, choosing what is in
each room, the layout, the doors, the
traps, where the Boss is hiding, and
more.
The GM can add in loot chests with set
credits or items inside.
The GM may choose to run the game in a
more "roleplay" style with added story
elements, non-player characters,
mission goals, etc.
In this way, the GM can use WI for all
reading, writing, and intelligence
based rolls. The GM may also use CH for
all social based rolls with NPCs,
enemies, and more.

Try playing the game on a traditional grid based game mat with miniatures. Each miniature can move 1-2 squares at a time orthogonally as part of the melee attack phase.

Ranged attacks may be made at a distance. Melee attacks may be made while adjacent.

Come up with your own house rules!

MICRO SCIFI RPG

CHARACTER RECORD SHEET

NAME: **RANK:**   **CLASS:**

STATS

ST   DE   WI   CH

PROFICIENCY:

WEAPONS

RANGED: **MELEE:**

ARMOR   ITEMS

WILL   HEALTH   CREDITS

61

Expand Your Adventure With These Stand Alone Micro Chapbook RPGs!

Find More World Building Options and Create Stronger Characters with these Micro Chapbook Supplements!

Made in the USA
Middletown, DE
04 July 2020

11915701R00038